FROM A GAEL WITH NO HEARTLAND

Written for, and dedicated to,

My Perfect Enigma.

FROM A GAEL WITH NO HEARTLAND

ALAN McLEOD

SCOTTISH CULTURAL PRESS

First published 1996

Scottish Cultural Press
PO Box 106
Aberdeen AB9 8ZE
Tel: 01224 583777 • Fax: 01224 575337

British Library Cataloguing in Publication Data
A catalogue record for this book is available
from the British Library

ISBN: 1 898218 62 5

Printed by Progressive Printing UK Ltd,
Leigh-On-Sea, Essex

CONTENTS

ALAN McLEOD

Alan McLeod is the most radical and perceptive poet ever to have emerged from the Highlands of Scotland. He is the voice of young Scotland and its beatless generation — the voice of the generation of Scots and Britons disaffectionately known as 'Thatcher's Babies'. Alan is a Highland rebel with a clearly focused and serious cause.

Alan's work is unique. Romance, affection, feminine perception, humour and beauty are set against an ugly backdrop of anger, frustration, tragic-Celtic-angst, brutality and grotesque profanity. *From a Gael with No Heartland* read aloud is addictive, shrouding the reader in a world of beauty and love, and transporting them on a journey of euphoria and peace. But in the middle of the dream, he kicks you in the face, breaks your heart, stabs you in the back and carves your forehead with the words he considers best describes us: DIDN'T LOOK, DIDN'T THINK, DIDN'T KNOW, DIDN'T CARE!

At only 29 years old, Alan McLeod is surely one of the most exciting Scottish writing talents of the decade. Born and bred amongst the crofting communities of East Sutherland, he was educated at Golspie High School and Robert Gordon University in Aberdeen, from which he graduated in 1987 with a degree in Business Studies and a Diploma in Marketing. He initially trained as a Chartered Accountant; qualifying in 1990. He left the profession shortly afterwards, and now commits increasing amounts of his time to his writing, his music and his poetry.

BECAUSE THAT'S WHAT DREAMERS DO

I look at your house, from a peaceful place
I close my eyes, I can see your face
Smiling
And I smile when I think of you
Because that's what dreamers do

I touched the wind and watched it play
Dusting your hair – take my breath away
Enigma
Perfection wrote a song for you
Dream of singing songs of love
Because that's what dreamers do

Emptied my eyes onto my thighs
Carrying this torch is no disguise
Enigma
What am I supposed to do
Just keep on dreaming dreams
Because that's what dreamers do

Kiss you each night when I go to bed
Hold your hand and I nurse your head
Enigma
I want to spend my life with you
I dream of eating you up each night
Because that's what dreamers do

No-one understands why I smile each day
But I understand – since you went your way
You can't kill thought
You just kill form
Take away the rain
And there's still a storm
Enigma
What are you going to do
If you want it
Then believe it
Then you can touch it
And manifest your dreams
Because that's what dreamers do

I dream we'll be together – dead or alive
Our spirits joined together in the after life
Enigma
That's what I'm going to do
Dream of dying alone
And in heaven, meeting you

Because that's what dreamers do

OLD MAN CHOPPY

You're the biggest farmer in the land
But I don't really understand
Why its me and my brothers three
Who end up chasing your bloody sheep
You have a collie – it cost a bomb
He loves the car – he can do no wrong
Can't you see as he lies asleep
Your collie canna gather sheep
Your Ranch is huge – a Texan's dream
As you drive around in your limousine
I'm not being rude, I don't mean to scoff
But I think you'd like to be a toff

You've come some way since you were born
And God blessed you – he did adorn
You with a weapon – but not a whopper
That's not why you're called John Chopper

In early days 'twas Gaelic folk
There was rarely ever English spoke
Until you met your teacher new
Who said he'd try to tutor you
A class of ten were taught new words
Your Gaelic tongue was never heard
Vocabulary increased – up ten fold
Before you were but five years old
He asked you for another word
Dreach is wet – a grouse a bird
And then he asked – what for rough sea
And John shouts out – please Sir, Ch-ch-choppy!

So here's to you – old man Choppy
The man who likes a wee, wee totty
They say you always liked a dram
From whence you ever left the pram
They also say that you are tight
Just like a ducks arse clamped in flight
So father please go buy a round
And mind you'll need more than one pound

Aye…you're a damn fine driver – we all can tell
You've driven to heaven – via hell
Your driving stories are awful funny
They always start with – 'When I drove for Sonny'
You drove down South – drove East and West
Sonny said you were the best
But for one weakness – one minor scar
You could never drive straight past a bar

You carried sheep – you carried cows
You even hauled a new kit house
But mind what happened at Loch Maree
You say you stopped just for a pee
The snow came down – kit house not covered
You told the barman – 'I'm not bothered
The joiners'll wait an hour or two
So a half an' a half an' a wee shaloo'
I suspect you knew there was a Ghillies' Ball
You didn't give a toss at all
A few days later you creeped back home
It took less time to build up Rome
But times were hard – you said 'I'm sorry
And the drifts that night were over the lorry
I had to stop – the snow was deep
I'd just one dram to get to sleep'

4

Your driving stories – I have to gasp
Just like the night at Willie Naast's
You boasted long about your skills
But you never made it up the hill
Leaving Naast's at half past two
You'd poured some whisky into you
'What do they know they're drivers not
They haven't got what Choppy's got'
Just as well – they've God to thank
They didn't end up down a bank
For a man who's driven near and far
You were fairly skunnered without a car

You drove for Baxters – a dumper truck
On Gruinard Hill to make a buck
Not one brake – the risks you'd take
Burning rubber – keeping Laide awake
But then one day – a mistake I fear
To the Gruinard cliff – you went too near
Jumping off in the nick of time
Your dumper rolling down declines
All you said was 'I..., oh, heck'
Today you still can spy the wreck
Baxters – glad you were alive
Gave you a barrow that you could drive

One more thing to say on driving
You worked out every way of skyving
When people talk of trips they make
You stand up straight and a breath you take
'Listen here boy – what the hell's a tacho-card
I've done more miles reversing than you've done forward'

You're a father too of four fine sons
Can you remember the names of every one
There's Robert, me, James and Pudding
Remember Pudding when he was screwing
He woke you up at half past three
'Hey Dad, any chance o' borrowing a johnny'
Embarrassment! to ask your Dad
And even worse – three packs you had

To wake you up is no mean feet
What with your snoring and smelly feet
You snore all night – the Bungalow shakes
There's not much more the walls can take
So thank God Rachel – you're taking him home
It's gonna be bliss without his drone
We've tried to stop him – we've all tried drugs
So I think you'll need my old ear plugs

And he's bad for thinking he's still a stud
In spring he's like the flowering buds
So don't get edgy if he starts to sweat
At 62 – his dreams aren't wet
But just in case – I went to Boots
Well at 62 – who gives a hoot
So I'd really like you to have this treat
To stop the pitter-patter of tiny feet

Last night the Best Man said to Choppy
'Will you be a man and make her happy
Or like a mouse wait 'til tomorrow
To get back from Pudding what he had borrowed'
Choppy replies to his best man
'My oldest son – you don't understand
This is fact – but not quite right
I'm just a rat – I was there last night.'

ODE TO A DREAM

Your beauty
Your smile
And your golden hair
Haunt me
And taunt me
And without a care –
I freefall into ecstasy

Tenacious
Contagious
And dangerous
Your aromas
Enslave me
And trade me –
for life's absurd reality

For I am the dreamer
I dreamed of you
And I lived my dream
On 842
My mind: pan-mundii
Found rest with you
A dream in a million
Has now come true

You talk
I listen
I held your breath
In my hands
I inhale
And find my rest –
In your warmth

Oh, pleasure
Such pleasure
You stole the pain
One second
One touch
I'm a man again –
in your heaven

For I am the water
The aqua man
I flowed in the air
For the earthy one
And, ah … you appear
Like a bolt from the blue
With steely eyes, oh …
Oh … I absolutely adore you

Herring boat with a sunset sail
And plasticine flags
Very sad fish
Very happy seagulls
Rusty mouths
Oxidised souls
Humped cat's back
Grant aided tractors
Empty litter bins
Littered paths
To our sartori
Shivering off our inner skin
Onto mother's earth
Cruelty creates wealth
Love destroys our dreams
Always looking for rewards
And flags of plasticine

Warning! nothing's safe
Dangerous moons
And ears of corn
Mama's faced the serpent
And lived to tell the tale
Of rivers and Peter Pan
Of avant garde wallpaper
Old Uncle Norman with his tobacco pouch
And pot-holing in Spain

Of leaping salmon
Of her old Chinese guru
Looking through
Glasgow windows
On rainy tenement days

And did you too see
The boy with the butterfly
On his erect cock
The yellow death
From the Black Forest in the Rockies
To vaginas in your Caithness flagstone

UP AT UPPAT

My father was a dairyman
My mother lifted eggs
My brothers slept 'til 6 a.m.
When I was out of bed
Bruising oats and feeding calves
And washing byre floors
When I look back, the backs that broke
Will never heal the sores

To Be In Gairloch

Here I sit, my head in my hands
A victim of my dreams and my well thought plans
No more sun, the heavy door has slammed
Oh, to be in Gairloch, lying on her sand

Here I muse, I muse of places seen
Never to be visited, dealt with by my dreams
Inside a hollow sycamore or a pretty summer scene
Oh, to be in Gairloch, lying on her green

Here I cry, careers all going astray
Ambitions cast from memories, goals all cast in clay
No more salary, no more pay
Oh, to be in Gairloch, on a sunny summers day

Here I sing, I sing of acid trees
I sing of Gaelic currency and a radiation breeze
No more traffic lights or contaminated leaves
Oh, to be in Gairloch, drowning in her seas

Here I girn, I girn at what I am
A pretentious little Hitler, stirring up a sham
No more anger, if I could find a calm
Oh, to be in Gairloch, a virgin in her palm

Here I'll die, I'll die unless I fly
Directly West to Achnasheen and on into the sky
No more cheating, no more lies
Oh, to be in Gairloch, my child, my wife and I

THINKING

Thinking of Corby makes me
Think of sawdust
Thinking of Dad makes me
Think of Luing bulls
Thinking of cows makes me
Think of clover and milk
Thinking of toilet doors makes me
Think of tippex
Thinking of Wendy makes me
Think of 98 miles per hour
Thinking of Bruce makes me
Think of Julia
Thinking of singing makes me
Think of Japanese whalers
Thinking of Greenpeace makes me
Think of the Dalgety's
Thinking of morris dancers makes me
Think of rusty grey vans
Thinking of sheep dip makes me
Think of Kintradwell
Thinking of tractors makes me
Think of Donnie Cummings
Thinking of my friend Donnie makes me
Think of you
Thinking of you makes mc
Think

TAX

Tax avoidance, tax evasion
The biggest pass-time in the nation
Kill the profit, loss creation
Screw the IT, screw inflation
Tax avoidance, tax evasion

Men with money
Men with power
Sitting in their ivory towers
Accounts won't balance
Accounts won't square
Screw the poor it seems so fair

Let's make losses
To hide our wealth
We never use the National Health
Let them suffer
Let them die
The poor can shout and scream and cry

Call the tax man
Get him round
Kick him when he's on the ground
Let him beg
For Tory mercy
Then he'll wear his fascist jersey

The company car
A Jaguar
They say the dodge has gone too far
So double it
Treble it
Tax the wheels of the Great Ol' Brit

Fill their chests with lots of money
The Chancellor
He thinks its funny
A Robin Hood
With a balaclava
Rob the poor for the rich, 'OK-YAH'

Prescriptions up
So drugs get dearer
Yet dopey Britain gets much nearer
And far away
The IRA
Cut the cake with the UDA

The stock exchange
Is full of crashes
Like the M1 and its smashes
Where dividends
And attached tax credits
Are pocketed by CA's debits

PLANS

Look!
Don't fool around
Get a job
Settle down
Buy a house
Buy some debt
Lease a car
Take a test

Listen!
Think ahead
In 50 years
You could be dead
Get insurance
A pension too
Plan for children
Two will do

Stop!
Watch my style
I use a map
For every mile
Plan ahead
Do as I
If you don't
You're sure to die

oh, fuck!
so will I

(whose fucking bright idea was this then?)

CORNTOWN

The green fields grip my goutted feet
Like adhesive and shit smeared arse
Wide wheeled tractors, empty trailers
Old straw bales and red, rust bailers
Flies and more flies, stumbling roads
Staring cows and fences with holes
And sister in law and sister in law
Everything I did, everything I saw
Kick me when I'm down, no sound
Not my way: in your stage play
Leave me alone in Corntown's fields
Dust, drystane, U2 and feel
The sun that burns and you, your hurt
With spotty skinned girn and sarc-
Asms make me spew on stone
In Corntown let me be alone

ALL FUCKED UP

I'm a fucked up man
With a fucked up plan
I'm swinging from a dead oak tree
On a fucked up rope
With fucked up hope
Where's Spiritus Mundii

I'm a headless corpse
With fucked up thoughts
With stars falling down on me
From a fucked up sky
From Loch Uissie high
I can see that fucked oak tree

I'm a piece of string
I dance and I sing
They laugh as my life slips by
On a fucked up haze
I'm a black brick maze
Don't care if I live or die

I listen to the man
With the fucked up plan
I listen and I mend his heart
I kissed his head
And I made his bed
His burden I take and depart

Who listens to me
When I have to be
The fucked up head in the sand
No-one, no friend
They all just pretend
An oak tree that no-one has planned

So this fucked up man
Has now found his plan
I swing from the dead oak tree
With a new nylon rope
My boots full of hope
I know that heaven's for me

THREE LITTLE PIGGIES

(a study of family and social dynamics)

There were three little piggies
All born pink
Each smelt funny
All swore like minks
Their daddy and their mammy
Were both piggies too
Who lived in a sty
That resembled a zoo
The three little piggies
Baby sows, they grew
From hand-me-down small trotters
To pretty, pink-bowed shoes
And into pretty dresses
Mummy pig did squeeze
Her little baby piggies
For all her friends to see
As the pigs got bigger
They all began to fight
Behind the red-brick steading
As pleased as pigs in shite
But the girny pigs victorious
Bullied middle sow
When they pushed her in the midding
You should have heard the row
The biggest pig, a bully
Would always kick and shout
Every time she made a grunt
She'd get right up your snout

And baby pig, so moody
The girniest little bore
Would trot off to her sty a-raging
And always slam the door
From middle pig, so peaceful
You'd never hear a sound
She always kept her snoutty clean
And well pressed to the ground
For she'd be snorting for some muck
The other two had missed
Especially in the hidden corners
Where someone else had pissed
But now the sows are pinker
Age has made them big
Into the world they wandered
In search of hunky pigs
The oldest pig has married
The youngest pig, almost
But middle pig, the quietest sheep
Has always ate the most
But of the three
Who would you choose
If given half a chance
To spend a life of misery
That's loosely called romance
Well some would say
'Loud snorting pig – that's the one for me'
Well I can tell you think again
Don't lose your liberty
Others chant, 'The moody sow'
The lightbulb's 'friendly' queen
Imagine sleeping in her sty
Its really quite obscene

For on the floor, a thousand pairs
Of dirty knickers lie
And in the summer when its hot
The sty is full of flies
But wait a while, what of you
The middle piggy sweet
The apple of your mother's eye
A model pig, discreet
You surely are the ideal pig
All pink with trotters clean
The vision of a thousand bores
In all their wettest dreams
Beautiful and sweet you are
Closer to my heart
Than all the other pigs on earth
Especially those who fart
But here's to you my perfect pig
With your curly little tail
You're like a pork chop undercooked
Juicy and quite rare

VICTORY

The moon goes down
On a barbed wire fence
As the floodlights choke
In a fog so dense
The station stirs
From its seedy sleep
Across its halo
The angels creep

All dressed in blue
So royal and red
The columns quiet
Are slowly led
From Highland seas
To victory
8000 march
For history

A pensive army
Kings and queens
Gospels and singers
In a carbon scene
A deity
Of the Bhudda man
Of the only coming
Of the County fan

DEAR MR FINLAYSON

I write
To tell you of my further plight
I've fallen off my mountain bike
Again, I've wraxed my knee

You may recall
You're treating me
The ligaments in my right knee
Have all but gone – abandoned me
In a rugby injury

My knee had swollen
But now its down
It remains quite stiff
When I walk around
Stable not
It wobbles too
This is why
I write to you

Please advise of what to do
My Donjoy's wearing out
An orthroscopy or a four wheeled bike
I'll leave it up to you

But call me on 0134
81-treble-2
To re-appraise my ligaments
And what they fail to do

Yours sincerely
Without a chance
Of winning now
The Tour de France

NOISE

If I were to go next door and speak
I would, this week
And tell them of my meek
And kindly heart

But I would have to calmly say
You spoil my days
With noisy ways
And sickening art

If they decided not to be
A silent family
Then violently
Their limbs apart

But if they chose a life serene
Then its a dream
A silent scene
Still, beating heart

WHO ARE YOU

What is it that keeps you from sleeping
Has beguiled your smile
And sent all this weeping
I understand not the look on your face
The cold empty stare
At whatever I say

Could it per-chance be
Loss of control
Of life as you knew it
Not knowing your soul

Your grip ever slipping
Past falling away
And I say 'sunshine!
start making new hay'

I sit and I wonder in silence
Into clinkers I stare

SLAVE TO THE GIRO

Pay cheques do not
A slave me make
Un agent libre
In Herr Greed's wake

All asunder
On the take
From the ark
You bilious snakes

THE GAELIC DREAM

Do you want to feed the language
Or feed your greedy minds
With futile dreams of victories
By chance or by design
Do you want to nurse your egos
Or truly save the Gaels
For if you did, you'd shut your mouths
And let the truth prevail

You're like old men, all gripping sticks
Without, you'd surely fall
Let go and let the young blood flow
Find your holes – and crawl!

The sun will rise up from the dark
Hopelessness will fade
Into the pit of petty fools
You dug and boldly made
But if you choose to hold us back
Your interests close to heart
Then dig your pit and make your bed
As this young Gael departs

You're like old men – a piobaireachd race
A clan without an heir
Defying our claims and Gaelic dreams
You pipe the devil's air

JUDAS

The Reverend sits in his white, white room
He knows the fishy cycle ends quite soon
His wife downstairs has seeds of doubt
She parts her curtains and looks straight out

She sees me walking 'long Lenaig Way
Her vicar husband knows not what to say
To mend a heart – pick up the parts
Tear up Epistles – a revealing start

Exodus, Acts and Kings
Abraham kissed his daughter's ring
Revelations, from Pete and Paul
Brother Judas – do you have balls

Judas drags me by the ear to church
If I sin will Satan come and hurt
And break my heart – I fell in love
I on my back and she above

Astrological books by my bed
Buddhism and Anarchy inside my head
Unstable – psychologically
Look in the mirror – who can I be

CEBIT

Oh Mr Junkie, can you not see
That effort is not all
As God once said
When all was dead
'How the mighty fall'

Like a dream
The more you chase
The further it will run
Unlike a snail
Effort fails
Life is simply fun

See your goal
A casual eye
You'll never, ever fail
Like a hammer
Made of air
You'll never beat the nail

HANNOVER BLUES

My love for you is like a yolk
It breaks my brittle back
As I plough, my plough share splits
My seed spills from my sack
Of jute and cotton and hardened cloth
I lay you down to sleep
A tear like jack-boot wipes my smiles
And happiness doth weep

Your ignorance of my heart's beat
Breaks both my souls in two
One splits clean; the other cracks
Like brittle, brown, brogue shoes
But on I strive to make you see
The error of my ways
For in this race of Hannover's lace
I count the blessed days

ROSS COUNTY

The sky is grey
The water blue
Ben Wyvis white with snow
You'll see our breath
As we raise a roar
And watch the County go

The Wizard winds
His wily frame
Around our enemy
Like lightening in
A gilded cage
He sets the County free

You could go
400 miles
To hear the Hampden roar
But o'er our bridge
You'll hear a roar
You've never heard before

Victoria Army
Proudly stands
Our troops of Royal Blue
Await the call
To go to war
To tame the mighty shrew

We will walk 10000 miles
We will swim the seas
We will rise into the sky
And follow our Ross County

ISLAND LOVE

A thousand eyes watched you tonight
As we danced beneath the stars
The jealousy that surrounds our love
Admiration from afar

We are the orchids among the nettles
The roses with the sweetest petals
Love's a tour of unknown pleasures
Of sunken ships and buried treasures

We danced on a Viking windswept moor
To the sound of a pictish wail
Our love is deeper than the soil below
And older than the Orkney tales

The sea that ebbs between these Isles
Has tides like my own heart's blood
With every smile and glint in your eye
Comes rushing my undrunk love

To the sun we turn like those before
As we settle on the shore
We worship love, like God herself
In heaven's Ring of Brodgar

MY MOTHER'S NO VIRGIN

The snow creeps down your mothering mountain's skirts
And your childlike knolls
Huddle close
Fearing
Their time will come

Hidden in mist
The top tablet of your head
Bears the wintry disease!

Sweeping past your splaying feet
Your filth bubbles and spews
Out unwanted waste
And in its blackening depths
I hear the cries of unwanted children

Young and innocent
I saw no wrong
A child with dreams
A child with songs
But now your rain
Stings my eyes
And I realise
It was wrong

Who's my father
What's these scars
I grew up sleeping
In Dingwall's bars
The dye's been cast
The damage done
My soul is septic
Mother

You're no virgin

MY CHILD

And I sat here young man
Alone
Among the rocks and fallen castles and fallen stones
And contemplated your future

To the sky I turned
And in its breath
I saw the wonder of love

Oh young man
your mother tried hard
She bent her back
and broke her bones
For you she saw no end
to her pain

Again and again and again
She cried
And I tried, in vain
To make her see
You were a son rebelling
Anarchy

But like the trees
You bent to please
And now
The strongest wind
Carries you away
To pleasures
To women
To sin
And we've lost you
Forever

TO THE GYPSY WOMAN

The saddest moment of them all
Is when our hearts try not to fall
Miles apart, aside a sea
Break of these chains and set us free
To rise above this shite and fly
To wrap our love up in the sky
Golden lace surrounds our hearts
No miles to tear our love apart
Our love is the strangest thing
Magnetise two human beings
Torn apart in sado-bliss
End this pain with but one kiss
A kiss so clear and pure I see
Us making love – eternity
Your smile inspires me everyday
For everlasting pink, I pray

I sit at night in empty rooms
Pouring heart in lamenting tunes
My meagre whistle moaning airs
Of heaven's steps and the broken stairs
Looking round this deadly place
All I see is my love's face
On every wall and through the glass
An image of today has passed
Everything of yours I touch
My stomach knots, my twinging crotch
Nursing wounds that grow so deep
I have no scythe, I cannot reap
So I just sit down here and cry
And ache because my love won't die
I worship you like morning dew
For Gypsy Woman, I love you

HEADBANGING TO BEETHOVEN

Friends, pray tell me
This dear fascination
You bestow
Does it make you go
Like an engine of steam
Or her
In my dirty dreams
Or does it seem
Strange
To think of it
i.e.
Headbanging to Beethoven

Friends
We all sit on beds
Or on top of our heads
Cats play with dogs
Beethoven with clogs
Banged out of the window
Into the night
Darkness his light
Or does it seem
Strange
Was Ludwig deranged
When he thought of it
i.e.
Headbanging to Beethoven

FROM A ROOM WITH NO VIEW

Far in the distance rocky peaks
Rising, a Highland plateau
This feeling of belonging
Did that placate my forefathers
Raised up there, chased down here
I've been in cities
I hate them
This I like best
First impressions

Common folk
Full of the Gael
They're warm and rainy
Like Lochinver hugging its plot
This Glasgow is just one act
Trans-humance without stops

I left this morning
Anger, cutting my throat
Slow, smelly, shining trains
Dragging me along
It would be easier to give in
Not to fight for home
But go South
No way
Not this Highlander

I can smell the despair
Highlanders smell when they come here
The trains, the bairns, Gaelic cameos
Your lucky you can take it
She said
Hate it and go

HELLO

Hello out there, somewhere
Far away in mist
I missed you last night
As you hugged your cannabis
A shadow cast by moons
Over your promise
That you will wait
How soon can I come in from the cold

Hello Picasso, a smile
Serenades those shadows
As I swallow mobile homes
Eat their filthy food and splatter
Of Academia caged
By their transparent skins
Hello Picasso
How soon can I come home

Hello home, rivers and breast feeds
Autumn smells swell this heart
And apart I roam
And I find myself an immobile phone
Calling the world, come and stay
Desolate heteros and smugly gay
They touch down soundly and roundly
Within 1.5 days, decide to go away

ISRAELITE

Israelites

Men of the sand
A tameless Jew on sunny nights
Fights for his sun
Remember he is the son of God

Pyramids and Knights
Creation of the land
Of the people
Of the hand of power
– its sand
A metal box where love
Weighed by clocks
A calendar sleeps
While on the rocks
The weak man falls
Is this why the Jew
Thrives on the sand

A blackened sin
Of love and hate
It was for her sake
That the white man broke her in
So quiet, yet oh so loved
An oppression of smiles

Don't tell me
You lie
Of the road when you rode
To the clouds and sang to God
I sinned
I laughed
The sand and the sun and the son
Cried
He is the one
O Mighty Israelite

PANE THROUGH A GLASS EYE

They've got us by the balls
But they can't hear us screaming
This can't be a nightmare
I'm not even dreaming
How can I wake up
There's no time for sleeping
Don't listen to me talk
You'll never catch me speaking

I'm out of this world
I've got no pockets
I've got no clothes on
Way out of this world
I can't have pockets
Without my clothes on
Way into my soul
This material thing
My rectum pockets
My sphincter ring

I'm drowning in systems
This is my inability
To get into the inner
To control my own destiny
I'll start walking on air
The path from creation
To the unblessed table
At my sane bus station

HOUSE OF HELL

I was drowned by that deadly weakness
My life, slowly gripped by death
Death, not of life, but love
How absurd
The war of love
The peace of fear

All things bright and beautiful
All good things come to an end

HOUSE OF HELL PART 1

That deadly weakness began to blind
Blind the sense staring me in the eye
All around in the house of hell
Lay a smell, a smell of death
I begged for help
No one turned

Harry Hall faced the wall
He didn't care
His heart was broke
He said fuck all
The thought of me
The man
Drowning, dying because of love
He laughed
If he talked, he would choke on his own vomit
He didn't care when I died
I will return to the House of Hell
To the House of Harry Hall

HOUSE OF HELL PART 2

Its hell in the House of Harry Hall
Where you don't hear a wind
But a breath
A breath scented with ancient blood
Blood belonging to me
Me is the ghost which now hells
Hells in the House of Harry Hall
I died of heroine pity
The druggie land of opium love
I flew high in the sky
Trying to land, land on the land
So I could rule the world
The world don't jive love junkies
I cried as I flew high in the sky
Flying higher and higher
High up to Hell
Hell in junkieland is up – not down
And in hell the junkie king
Over-powered with love and junk
Gave me two choices
Die in hell, in hell a love junkie
Or live a hell – on earth – a love junkie
I returned to no-man's land
I found nothing
They found it all
The abstemious and promiscuous
I don't understand

Its hell in the House of Harry Hall

TORCHES AND STICKS

See flickering lights across a moor
Like a mis-spent youth used to be
I see a man with a torch and a stick
Just like a mis-spent youth ought to be
Freedom for my people comes
In the strangest ways
This man with the torch and the stick
Used to say
But I know he was wrong
So I wrote a song
And we all rose up again

To fight
Stand up and fight
God be the witness of our peoples' plight
To tramp 'neath our feet the sons of men
Who'll carry the torches all over again
If we don't fight

I see a statue on a hill
Above a village with sand
Stones dragged by our people
With lashes on their backs
The leaders among those
Carried torches and sticks
Were so, so bold
But our people in their souls remain
To rise up again

To fight
Stand up and fight
God be the witness of our peoples' plight
To tramp 'neath our feet the sons of men
Who'll carry the torches all over again
If we don't fight

STATIONS

And even in this filthy station
I can imagine in the coldness
A movement of dirt
To reflect it all
On disinfected floors
Tickets, perfumed air and swinging doors
All around
Like a metamorphosis of sandy music
And rasping chord progressions
Is this what I dream of in a station
Or is it just a hard old station

Oft I have laid head in hands
To turn it around and flee this land
But aimless flies with intentions unseen
Surround me like the arse of a beast
Such is this pit, I am
As music rises the minutes pass by
Colours dulling and smelling
And all the time this mongrel life
Alive and breathing the dieseled air
Like pinkness in gin, the subtle unknown
For can I really resist
This hard old station

Like life itself it gets too much
Where from refuge we seek
Another
To a train of the same

The endless beat, for I can't find a heart
But on I struggle to see the end
In this perfumed world of locomotion
And diesel stains
Minutes, hours and lives pass in this hell
Release me soon, release me soon
The wheels just grunt to a shiny-arsed master
And in the mine the horses of steel
Are blind – but free

SWEET MIST IN MY PALM

And in this land
I see and hold a ragged view
Of heathened heather and ragged rock
Oh, give me home, land of dishonesty
Turn them out off my palm
Off the land and off our farms
Make way for our peace
Oh, stay sweet mist and turn
Them away from our midst
Sweet mist
In my palm of this ragged hand

My fingers stretch like fingers cold
Into fable and rhyme
Of times unknown
Our culture is lost
Not hidden
In the midst of mist
Down there
Stretch out sweet ragged fingers
And scale the quim of hope
Lap up the sweetness
And breathe the ragged rhymes of time
Desert harsh land and enslave
And know now
Sweet mist
Your place and mine
Both in the palm
Of this ragged hand

SERPENT

On distant shores
I cut and gore
With poisoned puss
I smile at whores
As I watch their business
Creeping on tar
They spit on their masters
With chaotic catarrh

In distant lands
I wash from my hands
Frost bitten oxides
Meagrely attempted homicides
The smell of AIDS-ridden backsides
Makes me vomit at my fireside
With the blackest of coal
The stones in my soul

In my own home land
I can quietly stand
With her hand in my hand
Like Jesus and the sand
But the serpent assured
That our folk aren't pure
As we slithered and lied
On the bleakest of moors

And today I lie
Beneath the bluest of skies
Polluted by noise
Of a murderous voice
Spouting with wings
Deterrents and smoke
To scatter them all
The Bosnian folk

For why is it us
They say its a must
To toy and to test
Their tragedy jets
On the virginal soil
Where the serpent has coiled
Since the bombs have all dropped
The fighting's not stopped

TEXT ON BEING TOOTHLESS IN SEATTLE

From this hilltop of mere accumulations of fear
Evaluation brings forth to my eyes
Inutterables of concrete and people
And leaves me in tears
I realise reality
In mornings of moans and muscular strains
Elasticated vanities receded from foreheads
And brows, they encroach
Singular liars and stairs
To heaven we go, alone
People restore eyebrows with pens
I restore ghosts and water-filled pots
Of sand and soil from palms
No coconuts land on infertile sand
Or here
Ascension of paper and catastrophic skies
I see and I realise reality
Above in the stars
Constellations of stars
And wonder-bras
I pray – goodbye to it all
Leather jackets and squinting of noses
No woman in this place would appreciate roses
Or gardens of doom
With thoughts of love and divorce
And, of course, revenge

American culture consumes this city
Sewers of systems, methods of maledom
White lines define lanes
Assume this again and reply
Goodbye to it all
Households of fortunes and spinning clothes
People become heroes with toes
Curled in guilt
Heroes are people who travel miles
To see others starve
One day I'll invest in a culture
Or a home
Unfold sweet redness
Tapes of data and gates of water
Remember – American situations
No matter, we do not alter
Rich windows and tea cake saloons
Dolphins and rodeos
Archdeacons of doom
Can taps run at a loss
Can you shut them down
Do not lecture me
You clowns
On Edith Piaf and sandy ideas
Split the wood and snap the stake
You are not Jesus
So shut up for Fuck's sake

INTO THE SEA

Fingers of black
Of grey
Of all colours
Which have escaped from the womb of man

And into the sea
And into the blue
And into the cold
And into you

And into the sea
He goes
Into deep clarity
And sincerity
He knows
An escape from the fingers
Of black
Of grey
Of all colours
Escape from the womb
From the mother
Is she Mephisto
Or just no-one
Is he no-one
Going into the sea

I tried to trap a tidal wave
Just like a piercing tear
But eyes like tears will open up
And materialise our fears

The sun won't shine in death's dark way
When the valley opens up its gate
The only thing that makes them live
Is the rays of love and hate

The only way to fall
Is to dance on the ground
And trip on that lady
Who has never made a sound
In twenty years

And go into her sea
And into her pink
Swim to be free
Go into her sea

CAMEL

To sing on the back of a rabid camel
To cry with a swan whose neck is assigned
To the fate of the world as the camel and master sang
To the death of the light and the end of our time

Free sunshine will fall like the rain on sweet gravestones
To the ground where 'neath lies the reek of the dead
Dark blinds the dull ears like a deafening silence
To the inner most lines of the scars in our heads

Like the rocks that protrude from the face of a holy man
His journey mere steps for the strife of mankind
The spirit of the world will live on past materialist
The journey of the spirit is love to the mind

CHANGES

Hat on head
Woollen scarf
Three string vests
All out of place
Shiny shoes that
Hurt his toes
Stockings hold no shape
Wears no shirt
He is so poor
Cigarette butts
One by two
What is life
He knows no more

At twenty eight
He is a loss
Financially deprived
Unlike most
But at last moment
When almost down
Save his soul
Who'd be so bold
Rich young girl
Very nice
Love and money
Pays the price

Now at thirty
Cigars no end
Cyberspacing
Spend, lend, spend
Money here and money there
Money always everywhere
Three piece suits
Cars and girls
Drinking wine and dine

THE OCTOPUS

Free from the grip of Octopussian peoples
The eight armed parasites
Unarmed in war
Hold the loaded case close to your head
Move your mind
Case chases dead
Field a war against the money
Retreat from the city
War's so pretty
Its such a pity
Straight from Egypt to Korea
Career in money can't be found
Free the money
Free the food
Free me from Octopus
Don't take the blame
There is no shame
Money fights and creates
Creatures from the landlord's womb
Womb paranoid of poverty
Foetus hard and sits on stools
Needs no food
Feeds on blood
Can the world be freed from man
Man who runs away from water
Fear the blood
And so to make his followers rich
He takes the creatures –
The Octopus

CORNER OF MY ROOM

I sit in my corner
The one over yonder
I sit there at night
Can't move from the light
From the window in my corner

They all try to tell me
That one day they'll sell me
Or because of my age
As part exchange
For a dummy in my corner

Oh I'm so quiet
In my ordinary life
My corner is my light
My corner is my life

So maybe at ten
Or twenty or thirty
When my life is half over
I'll vacate my small corner
'Cause the smell is so dirty

WORRY

Subjective thinking drives me wild
Diving deep to another time
Where worry drives and worry thrives
It chills the bone
It chills my life

Worry works like wanting ants
It kills your love and kills your wants
Worry stays, goes on and on
It blinds you like
A desert sun

The wildest worry in my life
Scars my brain
My mind's insane
It moans and screams and mars with pain
It feels like stones – its only rain

But in the end all things do die
And so will worry – it will cry
The everlasting death is nigh
Worry fails you – let it lie

AND YET, YOU!

How many times must my tears fall on this desert
How many clouds must cross the sky
I see a core in Everest
Like the core in myself
And yet, you scale me

For how many centuries must I retain this mask
Of poppies and crystals and spectrums of hate
I see a place in your heart
Like the heart in myself
And yet, you defeat me

How many bowls must I beg with in this poor street
How many lepers must I sleep with in this operatic fight
I see a disease in your mind
Like a disease in myself
And yet, you cure me

How many bones must I crush on this blackest anvil
How many chimneys must I attach to my head
I see a home in my heart
Just like the home of the dead
And yet, you live there

And yet, you
Scale me
Defeat me
Cure me
And live here
But do you love me

I see how many lives I must live in this life
To see a cliff edge collapse like love on the rocks
And yet, I know the light in your eye
As my mind bends high
Is too serene
For you to love me

HYPOCRISY

I've got a cock like a Shetland Pony
The reverend said to me
Bend over boy, this is called
Homosexuality

What! men and men and boys and boys
What about the sheep
He blessed me with his bibled rod
His secrets I would keep

He talked of heathens, of men who drank
Women walking streets
Blue Peter never taught us how
To wank between the sheets

Oh, Valerie Singleton, what a dame
I thought that you'd be mine
But reverend bender said to me
This was the devil's sign

Hypocrisy, hypocrisy
You all stick in my throat
Establishments, come church and school
The police, the press, the goats

This is the Highlands' own cold war
Young against the old
Beatless generation rise
Or let your souls be sold

THE FUC

I can't try anymore, I can't see
One straight deal in The FUC
Are you all corrupt; or is just your style
To waste the cash in your baby's piggy bank
And blow it on the piles and piles
Of flower beds, trips to Brussels and football stadia
Who'll admit to that on Moray Firth
Our probing radio
Who'll stand up and say – 'sorry its me
Who wasted £16.5m at The FUC'
Is there one honest man or woman there
If there is, come out from under the stair
I've lost my faith in you, FUC
Where the fuck's democracy
Where a clerk of works has no work
But gets paid for sitting on his arse
Whilst impoverished children and pensioners freeze
Its a farce, you hear me, a fucking farce

And what of Objectives and the Internet
Are you all still muddling in that yet
Pudding lovers and black bulls grow
Fat, as our Council Tax and rates keep flow
Leadership, what leadership, you steer a rudderless ship
Your a captain with a tart to see in a far of port
That we need not visit
Or is it a Fort
The fourth you quietly built
To generate the hype
And propagate the guilt

And when you read this shall you say
He's mad, a liar, take him away
Well if I'm mental, Institutionalise
Oh I forgot, its Community Care
You don't sympathise
'Cause you're
The FUC

MAMA FRIEND

Your little shadows are
the shape of things to come
And as you enter now
the fruit of life you've spun
Your golden hair and years
upon you gracely lie
A mama's honeyed smile
lights up my sunset sky

I'll always want your hugs
on festive frosty nights
And prison walls alone
will never lock inside
This loveless soul apart:
apart and dis-embraced
I serve my prisoned hell
with memories of your face

Your heart's as big as God's
you shine on peachy moon
Utopia I met
inside your greening room
A palace, whispering trees
and leaves – the wind lies still
My ghost sings slow and sadly now
upon your weathered hill

The prime of life awaits
sewn – now shall yea reap
Take my proffered hand
and with it shall yea keep
A piece of broken heart
whose peace you helped to find
I kissed your rainbow's end
and tossed the gold behind

For life is just a wake
left in all our seas
Yours – the deepest ocean
into streams the Three
Springs of life anew
pure and snowy doves
Doreen – my mama friend
I thank you for your love

FORT GEORGE

You big, ugly bastard
Squatting like a washer wifey
Shitting in my sea
How can it be – you're still here
And my people still aren't free
To blow the skirler
Or work the croft
To fish the river
Or mine the rock
This is our destiny
In tears

With your dungeons dark and dreach
Like an untamed woman
Out of reach
Your clitoris dangling into my salt
My salty fluid where dolphins swim
With retarded fins
Pour out of your quim
Swimming in our shite
Tonight
I saw our destiny
In tears

The yacht slips sweetly, slowly by
Your walls of blood
Built brown and high
And beachcombed tubes make you
And I, cry – for the years
The years that passed for each lost cause
In history's log, the shortest pause
Who the fuck was Charlie
Who the fuck am I
But aye, tonight
I see my destiny
In tears

DOLPHINS

Well its half past eight on Friday night
I should be pissed by now
But someone with a dolphin crush
Has dragged me to the crowd
Of ogling dolphinologists
Beachcombing binocularazzi
I dared ask what the fuss was for
They stoned me like a Nazi

The Binocular Brigade
Staring out to sea
Neptune, mermaids or Moby's dick
Their effervescency
Fails to stir my loins
For fins I cannot see
Sitting playing my old guitar
Is where I want to be

But when I'm in that pub tonight
Ten Murphys in my gut
Its then I think of dolphins
As I hit the hut
My pants pulled down, my guts I drop
And out into the sea
Those poor dolphins have no choice
But eat me for their tea

Ten pints of Guinness, 13 Grouse
And one Korma washing down
When you spy the dolphins now
You'll understand their frown

The poor wee things have swallowed all
Including condoms filled
And panty liners
And Tampax towels
That soaked up all you spilled

So spare a thought for dolphin blue
Next time you flush the pan
Eating shite and drinking spunk
Is not the Master's plan

Responsible, responsible
We all must play a part
For if we don't, one day we'll find
Our World will fall apart

HOW THE MIGHTY HATH FALLEN

I read in print a tale today
A tale of love, of sex and play
Of lies, deceit and laboured loins
Of Lordly lust and gracious groins

An heir indeed, true to his creed
Fortunes free and free to breed
With wife and maid and all alike
Beneath sweet silk, behind drunk dykes

And sitting sad, The Lady weeps
Her tears fall fast in draps and dreeps
She dries her cheeks with satin cloth
She wallows deep in rotten wrath

Maid's father says in tones well kent
My daughters right, if fortunes spent
On making my wee meagre baby
Into a toff and second Lady

He's right enough as dung he flings
For bulls' dung doesn't buy big rings
For only wealth passed down in trust
Can buy a crofter's daughter's lust

So here's to you dear Lord don't fail me
Your common wife will never fail thee
For she is but a bit of beef man
To lay your horny, hairy hand on

Dear Lady, sorrow rapes my eyes
You can't sleep for baby's cries
But in your absence what's he to do
In a land with sun but without you

BUNCHES OF GRAPES

A bunch of grapes hang from this arm
Heavy, limp and ripe
The frustration in this man's mind
Is drunk, like the wine
What a cure

Labouring, sweating, collars choke
Nothing moves this lifeless limb
How can it hang there
Like bondaged bones
Blue bloodlessness blinds this man
His heart heavy
Feathery frustration firing tears

In depression these grapes don't move
Hanging like corpses cured
Infinitely preserved in a perverted state
Let us into your heart
It means much more than limbs
Limp and lifeless
I can see your heart is beating
Keep trying

We all line up – salute our limbs
In bottles we drown; but wine
This bunch of grapes
A bastard alien maybe
But its yours
Oh bunch of grapes breath
Be alive

ODE TO A WEALTHY WOMAN

The sun hath dawned to raise thy head
And lift thy body from thy bed
A frosty window traps thy thoughts
As thee touch the wealth thou wildly sought

From

Inside a world that caged thy heart
Whence sleep and dreams were torn apart
Thou sprang like water, pure and clear
To flow into a new career

To

Horizons howling with doors awide
Thou wait for no man, time nor tide
To struggle on with starry eyes
To show us all that thou were right

And

So here's to thee, I'll drink my fill
And cast away my poisoned quill
For success be great or be it not
I'll always hold thee in my thoughts

VIN A 'DERF

Let me tell you of a fine old wine
Sweet and kind and a friend of mine
Ageing slightly, its beauty refined
A classic '37, one of its time

The label deceives the youngest of eyes
Its maturity hidden as the aromas arise
For deep in its breath sweetness smoothes the air
And all around we find tranquillity there

A wine for warriors to sip at war
A wine for heroes to herald their cause
A wine for men the richness to taste
A wine for angels and God's own grace

Uncork it and feel it
That seediest of spirits
That rises from the neck
And takes Utopia with it
To a world where we all just stand in a line
And wait for the meaning whilst tasting the wine

But let me tell you this fine old wine
Is a wondrous woman, God would define
Her kindness and heart are larger than life
Vin a'derf made one man a wondrous wife

WHAT HAPPENS WHEN YOU TAKE
CARL JUNG SERIOUSLY

The window sweats
With heat and pain
As my sombre sleep
Breaks rusting chains
That moor, that soul
In Carl Jung's dreams
As water trickling from Highland streams

My Alchemist appoints the sane
To stir the acids in my brain
To curve perception
To crush my view
Awaken me
Awaken you

MILLTOWN CEMETERY

The graveyard grass was grey and matted
And flattened
By the feet of a Catholic crowd
Around the plot distorted puppets
All to suffer
Mourned death aloud with Banshees proud

The priest begins his sombre reading
Some reading
To the dead, for death they'd die, they did
The sacred bodies smirk in wonder
So sombre
They bite the bullet and close the lid

On wailing wenches who stir the skies
With cries
With grief the rain bestows a farce
And all around we realised
Close their eyes
That hate was great, and love was sparse

And in the distant haze he giggled
And wriggled
How dare they mourn their killers crass
And from his breast he hurled the bullets
Bombs and guns
To watch them slither through the grass

The IRA they chased in anger
With vengeance
And tried to squeeze the Orange dry
But from the woodwork come the Police Force
What a farce
To nurse the Orange and stop their cry

Just another day at Milltown Cemetery

GOD'S COUNTRY

In Caledonia, I

Walk out in the morning mist
Dew drops on my eyelids
Sunrise, sun shines
I kiss the ground that God has kissed

Waterfalls and flower showers
Golden sands and ivory towers
Rain clouds and rain falls
Every minute, every hour

In Iraq, I

See the armies, bombs and guns
Shining in the desert sun
Women crying, sons are dying
Is this God's country or is this the one

THE HEARTLAND

See Ben Wyvis rising high
Watch the golden eagle fly
See the rivers, streams and sea
See the stag, he wanders free

The Kildonan Strath still smells of smoke
The eastern coast still smells of hope
On the waters edge, Utopian pools
Spilling over with murderous wool

God bless Rogart and all its heirs
We all left home and no longer care
The old men die and take their graft
They laughed last with the longest laugh

On the streets of hell as the A9 plies
Its trade of death our libellous lies
In market stalls and Brora's tarts
The dream of home will soon depart

God save Golspie and all its sins
Before I walk between my kin
The gas works gone, roots eschew
On Sunday morning, the bells ring true

YOUR CHILD HANGS FROM A TREE

Young men!
You are scared of fate
Yet, you're aroused by a band from Skye
But when you're faced by a Lowland man
You run away and hide

You sit and watch your children grow
Surrounded by Lowland blood
When they're up, its much too late
As they're trampled in the mud

It is your duty
It is your child
You need to heed your history
For if you turn you back on truth
Your child hangs from a tree

IN THE YEAR OF THE PIG

I switched on my Hollywood lamp tonight
It was bright
I saw Orwell dance across the wall
I didn't understand at all
The TV message and the kicks
In the Year of the Pig

This guy hides in a skin of sin
Do you think he knows – Ho Chi Min
I don't – FBI don't want my eyes
Looking at those VCs die
I see the VC wound the hound lick
In the Year of the Pig

Johnson tries, I try, the world tries
Bhudda stops trying
The Vet cries as he recalls it all
The sin, the evil, the village walls
Burned, dressed in flesh he's sick
In the Year of the Pig

This TV sends shadows through my hair
Redgum, Nineteen, they've tried, I stare
'Dad, tell me about it', I say
He doesn't really know
He doesn't really care
That VC, looks like me, being kicked
In the Year of the Pig

The light burns my back
As I attack
The logic of the man
Who drove us along
To kill and destroy
The youngest of boys
On both sides of a parallel
Chinook and mortarshell
We have to exceed
A conscience with need
To ask the insane
Over again
Why did you do it
In the Year of the Pig
A boy like me could do it
In the Year of the Pig

PLOUGHMAN

And did you hear
The wind upon the sea
As we lay
In our stormy beds
And was it fate
That took your hand
And put it on my head
Or was it fate

And did you see
The ploughman's pair
Standing
In the stable bare
They miss him now
As the rusty plough
Will turn a rig
No more

And did you know
That you can break my heart
If you leave me
In this way
For the world
Is such a lonely place
I pray to God
That you will stay

So fare thee well
My ploughman friend
I will rock myself
To sleep
As the rain
And wind call out your name
I cry farewell
My ploughman friend

CHURCH

Its time to go
Its time to leave
What the fuck's
Inside your sleeve
My mama kept
A tissue free
Just in case
She had to sneeze
In church

W.E.G.

I love your smile
I love your hair
If you don't love me
I don't care

Because

When you smile I sing
The I.G.Y.
And when you cry, I'm
The Nightfly
Breezy weather and teaspoons pink
W.E.s and G.s this tink
Parrots ying and yang
Faganisms – tu es ma chanson

I sing

Empty me, oh empty me
Mind and soul et al
Circa 1967
We joined this human brawl

OFF MY TROLLEY

I knew things were bad
When I went mad
I didn't even have a name for myself
I didn't even have a fence
All I had was a wall
To kick
Against which I could wear
The toes out of my shoes

And nothing happened
For months and months
And then everything happened
All at once

Even the old horse chewed
My new checked jacket
I talked to myself and we sounded
Unhinged and Bracket

And my Rogart friend held peats so black
Enthusing from his new peat stack
Another's Moroccan, squeezed the oil
I just licked my lover's soil

But then I measured the man
By the height and colour of his tombstone
I drained his Sweetheart cans
And danced upon his grave bones

And it must be time, please God send
I'm ready for life's last long bend
I've eaten love and passed out friends
I've gone insane, this is

The end

Other books of interest from Scottish Cultural Press

Scottish Contemporary Poets Series
(for further details of this series please contact the publishers)

Gerry Cambridge, *The Shell House;* 1 898218 34 X
Jenni Daiches, *Mediterranean;* 1 898218 35 8
Valerie Gillies, *The Ringing Rock;* 1 898218 36 6
Kenneth Steven, *The Missing Days;* 1 898218 37 4
Brian Johnstone, *The Lizard Silence;* 1 898218 54 4
Siùsaidh NicNèill, *All My Braided Colours;* 1 898218 55 2
Ken Morrice, *Talking of Michelangelo;* 1 898218 56 0
Tom Bryan, *North East Passage;* 1 898218 57 9
Maureen Sangster, *Inside/Outside;* 1 898218 65 X
Anne MacLeod, *Standing by Thistles;* 1 898218 66 8
Walter Perrie, *From Milady's Wood;* 1 898218 67 6
William Hershaw, *The Cowdenbeath Man;* 1 898218 68 4

John Buchan's Collected Poems,
Andrew Lownie &W G Milne (eds); 1 898218 47 1

News of the World: Last Poems, Maurice Lindsay; 1 898218 32 3

Canty and Couthie: familiar and forgotten traditional Scots poems,
Anne Forsyth (ed); 1 898218 04 8

The Democratic Muse: Folk Music Revival in Scotland,
Ailie Munro; 1 898218 28 5